The Captain's Swallow

ANDREW WATERMAN was born in London in 1940. After six years working at miscellaneous clerical and manual jobs, he read English at Leicester University. From 1968 to 1997 he taught at the University of Ulster. His first collection of poetry, *Living Room*, was a Poetry Book Society Choice in 1974. Subsequent collections, all published by Carcanet, include two Poetry Book Society Recommendations and, most recently, his *Collected Poems 1959-1999* which gathers and augments the work in his previous books. He edited *The Poetry of Chess*, and has written a great amount of critical prose in the form of reviews, longer articles and book-chapters. Andrew Waterman is a recipient of the Cholmondeley Award for Poets. He now lives in Norwich, making prolonged stays in Sicily. Andrew Waterman's website is at www.andrewwaterman.co.uk.

ANDREW WATERMAN

The Captain's Swallow

CARCANET

First published in Great Britain in 2007 by
Carcanet Press Limited
Alliance House
Cross Street
Manchester M2 7AQ

A CIP catalogue record for this book is available from the British Library
ISBN 978 1 85754 886 0

The publisher acknowledges financial assistance from Arts Council England

Typeset by XL Publishing Services, Tiverton
Printed and bound in England by SRP Ltd, Exeter

For Guy Guiffrè and Paolo Pilato

e il naufragar m'è dolce in questo mare

Acknowledgements

Acknowledgements are due to the editors of the following, in which most of these poems first appeared: *Acumen*, *Critical Quarterly*, *The Frogmore Papers*, *The Interpreter's House*, *The London Magazine*, *PN Review*, *Poetry Review*, *Stand*.

Contents

In the Tyrrhenian Sea

This is how it must have felt to Odysseus:
one after another the islands rising from water,

Stromboli streaming out lava, next Panarea
around which sea gurgles with gases, then twin-peaked Salina

where the fleshy Aeolian caper grows, that some claim
is the land of the sirens; past Lipari's towering cliffs

(far islands two tents pitched on blue), we swing between
rock-fangs and fuming Vulcano, on up to landfall...

Though mine is no skiff with one sail, but pounding beneath me
the ferry from Naples. And he blew in from the east.

If these were his islands. All efforts to chart him founder.
In Homer the isle of Aeolus keeper of winds

has *sheer rock cliffs*, but it is *a floating island*...
Mariners then were returning with tales made taller

in telling, sorceries, shepherds who'd chased them away
transfigured into gigantic one-eyed Cyclops...

Still potent, the wonders. Ripe medlars cluster my terrace,
at the Marina platforms go up for a televised

fashion parade, *La Notte delle Sirene*.
My senses are rocked again by the scent of the broom.

Stromboli

This is the thoroughbred: immemorial
'torch of the sea', lighthouse for mariners,
by day its plume telling wind-strength, direction.

Dotted above the jetty are flat-roofed
holdings, white among palms and wisteria,
with vineyards and olive groves.

My road winds up to where shops and bars cluster
to a piazza ledged over sea,
where sipping a coffee I glance up

at the yellowish bell-tower solid above them.
Dwarfed by, above it, the summit
that now and again sends all packing.

In darkness, engines off, off the west coast,
no sound but a lapping of water, we wait,
all faces uplifted... 'Aaah...'

flame-gush, sparks hover then quench down Sciara del Fuoco.
A few minutes later, again
it gouts out lava and fiery debris...

As after a third and most brilliant gasp
from the planet's core we accelerate off,
I hear in stunned homage, 'Unearthly!'

Mr Carnival Bounces Back

Now they are at it in broad daylight:
with pastepot and brush where an alley dips to the Corso
the beaming features of Burro, Doddo, Pino,
Carnevale, Cincotta, Marmora, Nano,
are effaced by the smile and slogan of Bartolo Ziino.
The activists nod at their work, scamper off.
Candidate Carnevale will bounce back.

It is the election for the Provincial Council
of Messina, whereunder fall the Aeolian Islands.
And there are so many parties, their posters plastered
in Lipari town on all possible walls,
around the island, at Lami, at Quattropani,
and the other islands. On churches, on wayside waste-bins.
The conflict seesaws: up or down
each morning are Doddo, Nano, Burro, Ziino,
Chiara Georgianni (the only woman) and Pino.
Avvocato Carnevale always bounces back.

Another night's work, again his thick lips
in a clean sweep: three rows of twelve of him
at via Roma, via Franza, Marina Corta.
Vulnerable, true, to his rivals' pastepot hirelings –
but can they pay for so many posters?
Marmora, Pino, Cincotta, Burro, Ziino,
have bit-parts merely in these mural medleys.

There are business interests. 'No, not mafia,
not exactly,' Marisa tells me, 'men with influence.'
At the south tip of the island, from the wall
of the Observatory (a converted watchtower)
Mr Carnival (times a hundred) scans the cosmos.

He was a young *avvocato* when, in the sixties,
tourists first came, to save the islands' economy.
The grateful *liparoti* decided to feast them.
'Do not,' counselled Carnevale, 'ply them with octopus,
swordfish, squid. Offer them something exotic.
Gateau!' He had to explain:
'No, not *gatto*,' cat, 'but a rich French *torta*.'

11

So they bought many kilos of potatoes
in order to make more *gateau*, and more cheaply,
rigged up a hall with bunting and coloured streamers,
and invited the tourists. Who, when at last
the potato-gateau was cooked, got scarcely a morsel:
Mr Carnival was wolfing the lot.
So the local youth, to rebuke his discourtesy,
took down the paper streamers, stuffed them under
his chair, and ignited them: whoosh!
But Mr Carnival bounced back.

'His family,' Guy tells me, 'had a car
when most of us still rode donkeys. They would remove
each year for the three hottest months,
as the smart set did, to the heights of Pianoconte,
six kilometres above the town.
Then he inherited land in Calabria.
He came back on the *nave* with a battered suitcase
crammed with 500,000-*lire* notes.
A strange way for a lawyer to transfer a fortune.'

Carnevale's party, Alleanza Nazionale,
are *alla destra*, but no, they are not fascists –
fascist parties are not legal in Italy.
Gli eoliani votano un eoliano
reads his poster-slogan. 'That is,' says Guy,
'"Donkeys vote for a donkey."'

Now Mr Carnival plans a further party.
Vi invito, a poster in shops (including Guy's:
'I am a democrat, it is free speech'),
I invite you to Piazza San Cristofero
at Canneto for an evening of music, dancing,
and refreshments. Avv. Carnevale.

A sweep round the bay from Marina Lunga, the tunnel
cut through the great lava promontory, a twirl
of road, and here is the *lungomare*
of Canneto, under a gibbous moon.
And such scoffing and quaffing! Yes, I partake,
and a girl in jeans cartwheels around the piazza,
while another, backed by guitars, sings *Il ballo twist*:
Let's-a tweest again like-a we deed last summer,

Let's-a tweest again like-a we deed last-a year...
Mr Carnival rises to speak,
wearing a suit and tie, flashing his teeth...
But God, perhaps, is not an Aeolian
or, if he is, votes Doddo or Nano or Pino.
The heavens open: a downpour, thunder, lightning.
We are all put to flight.

Mr Carnival bounces back. *Vi invito* etc.,
to Marina Corta, takes over the Café du Port.
And when, after feasting and music and dancing,
he rises to speak, it seems God has relented,
we listen beneath a tranquil night sky.
'I promise you nothing' (orotund tones, florid gestures)
'that I will not deliver. For the young,
campi sportivi... And, for the old' – this and that.
'For our fishermen – seas full of fish.' Next, Education.
Aeolians must be graduates! For Canneto
a university... For Acquacalda
an airport, and for the donkeys of Alicudi,
autostrade...' I look up,
and the Man in the Moon winks back.

Carnevale is elected.
'We *liparoti*,' Guy's arms fling out,
return to roost on his brow, 'are *idioti*!
What were we doing when the rest of Italy
had the Renaissance, da Vinci, Raffaello,
Tiziano, Michaelangelo?
I will tell you – being beaten-up by the Turks
and dragged away in their ships into slavery!'
He glances across the Corso: 'Avvocato!
Avvocato Carnevale, *venga qua!*'
The politician bobs across
from the thronging *passegiata*, clad now in shorts
and vivid open-neck shirt, is bronzed from the sun.
Guy introduces me in rapid Italian
as 'your greatest admirer, at all your meetings,
who only laments that his vote is confined to England...'
Mr Carnival flashes his teeth, pumps my arm –
and before I get back a word rejoins his companions,
bouncing away like a beachball along the Corso.

The Golden Rule

Sunday, and the island
flocks to the beach at Canneto,
picnics and parasols along the pebbles.

March is early for tourists:
just one German treads gravely among them
stooping for shells.

'*Vieni qua!*' Come here!
yell the fathers and mothers, and
their children completely ignore them,

chasing each other in widening circles,
splashing into the water,
obeying their golden rule:

Out there! Out there!
whatever may be encountered.
Sea-wrack, rocks stuck with gastropods,

sea-tomato and sea-spaghetti
they locally call them;
or staring at poisonous jellyfish

(the Italian word is *medusa*).
Too young to be petrified,
to imagine risk.

World Crisis in the Aeolian Islands

Having flung my French windows wide to carry my coffee
out to the terrace canopied by flowering
bougainvillea, I turn back and flick on TV:
night sky is blossoming over Kabul.
'L'attacco! L'attacco anglo-americano!'
It has begun; but they have no details.
More bombs explode; outside more petals flutter
down. I breakfast, sweep up the pink harvest.
Still on low boughs their profusion seems undiminished.

Here, blue sea to boundless horizon;
Germans trawl the Greek theatre-mask collection
in the museum, grapes ripen to picking.
Karen is off to Palermo, 'fed up with drinking and sunburn'.
'Buon giorno!' – il Capitano, waddling along the Corso
wearing the same yellow shirt, or another one.
He eyes my boots: 'Good walking!'

It is. And as always away from the coast,
steep. Engines off, scooters freewheel past me,
I pass the Chiesa Maria dell'Annunziata
perched on its skew of steps. At Quattrocchi the view:
a savage west-coast sweep to rock-fangs jutting from water,
then the swart hulk of Vulcano,
lopped like a boiled egg, issuing poisonous vapours.

The reek of a fumarole somewhere behind me
I gaze out at Filicudi and Alicudi
humped on the sea, and settle among the broom,
Leopardi's 'lover of sad abandoned places'
that he saw when, raising his gaze through the broken columns
at Pompeii, he lambasted the vainglory
of his own age, and thought of unending galaxies
to which not only man and the earth, but the whole
sum of our stars are either unknown, or appear
a misty point of light, as they are from here.

Hubris raised the Twin Towers, and has erased them.
Our planet spins, the blue I stare into
lapsing out of sight does not comprehend
New York's grief, where dawn has not yet broken;
nor tonight's bombs raining on Kabul.

On Vulcano

1

At its last gasp, they say. The ancients steered clear
of its swart serrated cliffs, recorded eruptions,
and dedicated the island to their fire-god.
Gasp it does: the rotten-egg smell hits you
as the hydrofoil doors swing open, over the little port
the Gran Cratere sulks out its vapours.

At the turn into the climb, a sign with skull-and-crossbones
and in four languages: *Do not go near the smokeholes
extreme danger of intoxication...* Cinders at first,
sliding from under my boots, above the scatter
of gorse no shade, below me a sweep of landscape
dotted with farms growing olives and capers. The route
twists up red tufa furrowed as if some giant's
crazed corduroy, brinking the drop.
From the crater
a choice of views: out on blue rest the other islands;
within, compelling my gaze as its plumes rise past me,
I stare down into the maw of a planet.

2

Convicts, they lived in caves, drank from one foetid well,
mined sulphur, alum, staining them many colours
at the smokeholes. Lighting pipefuls against the fumes,
they died from them, or in knife-fights over the prostitutes
shipped across from Lipari.
United Italy,
having no use for the island, sold it to a Scotsman.
Mr Stevenson paid his work-force, built brick shelters,
bridged a chasm to speed his mule-trains down.
The electric telegraph came, connecting Vulcano
to what (as if this were not) we call the world.

Archduke Luigi Salvatore of Austria preferred
islands to courts. He details inch-by-inch
the Aeolians' terrain, plants, buildings, occupations.
remarking occasionally 'a stupendous view'.

In his volume on Vulcano, on facing pages
lithographs illustrate the Gran Cratere
before and after (a sweep of rim blown away)
it buried Stevenson's work, and dwellings and fruit-groves.
It is 1892. The Archduke is moved:
'Only children playing among the cinders break
a scene of abandonment filled with infernal squalor.'

3

Come to the mud baths, just follow your nose at the port
round the back of the honey-coloured fissured crag.
The islands' brochure, *Ospitalità in blu*,
commends their cure for 'degenerative diseases,
arthritis, eczema, gynaecological ailments'.

In blue they are not, fun-freaks, kids in for a dare,
trippers, maybe a few true believers with stabbing joints,
immersed indistinguishably, caking each other's faces
in the khaki broth. Don't go in with your watch on;
Silvia's handbag came out like a drowned rat.
This is as in Dante's *Inferno*; but his souls are sinners,
prodded under by demons, these shriekings are merry,
they scamper to rinse where a fumarole boils from the seabed.

Fretted with lava-juts, leaching saffron and orange,
wheezing mud-spurts, frilled and fringed with grottoes,
this island is Tennyson's Kraken that 'latter fires'
stir from the deep, 'by men and angels to be seen
In roaring he shall rise, and on the surface die.'
Latter to angels, and geologists;
to us a slow death. Meanwhile on its flanks
cling bars, the Benessere Beauty Center, Disco Pyro Pyro.

In the Museum

Framed by tall window
a hydrofoil arrows away
trailing a curve of foam
across blue below.

Around me in this room
rest artefacts made by
the island's first settlers:
weapon-heads, tools, blades,
fashioned from obsidian
spewed by the volcano;
pots with incised decoration.

All that survives of them.

The ship is gone from the frame,
the long white weal of its wake
dissolving like the millennia
back into sea. As they saw it,
fishing their life from it.

Cosmic

Looking at stars is looking back into time,
at what they were when they sent it, and conversely
anyone out there looking at us would not see,
here for example (allowing them zoom-in technology
aeons ahead of us) beach-towels and boutiques,
windsurfers, windscreens, Bar Trionfo, Trattoria del Vicolo,
be bowled off their feet (or whatever supports them) by
our thinking-up velcro, set wondering what on Earth
bikinis, bell-towers, garlic and goalposts are for.

But depending on light-years distance they might see
the ancient Greek theatre masks now in the Museum
up in the Castello back on performers voicing
their tragedies, comedies, a couple of millennia
before ramparts were built around their acropolis.
Or Stone Age craftsmen trading obsidian arrow-heads
all over the Mediterranean. Or much further back,
have a ringside-seat as cacophonous fiery ventings
heaved these seven islands up out of the sea.

I don't know if you've love, or guilt; but I send you a wave,
and an image you'll recognise, universal and timeless:
two workmen are struggling to carry, flat and side-on,
a door up too-narrow railed steps to my apartment.
'To the left!... No, to the right!' my landlady yells,
and they jiggle and juggle and jam it, at last realising
tilt it to upright; and as they attain the terrace
it smites branches, and pink petals cascade and it tumbles
clattering back down the steps to where all this started.

Dark Matter

'I have just had four women.' The gleam of white teeth is Franco,
strolling to where I sit on the low harbour wall
across from the parasoled tables where drinkers are chatting.
From the Castello perched on its great prow of cliff,
where the fireworks have ended until the next *festa*
(tomorrow perhaps) the Cathedral chimes down midnight.

'Over there,' he explains, 'I talk with four English women.
I say "Shall we go on to a disco?" They take out diaries,
check appointments, what they must do. I am Mediterranean,
here we say *Andiamo!* – Let's go! So rather
I will talk with you.' Franco likes to practise
his English. So he can go to Australia.

You can buy an abandoned farm dirt-cheap, do it up,
'Just a few forms to fill in,' said Janet, walking me
up brink-hugging overgrown mule-track to hers. Wall-fragments
no longer joined, I sprawled on 'the sofa', through rusted
springs grass tickling my face. 'For my art,' said Janet,
'You see the stars here, like nowhere back in the States.'

Or Sydney. *Andiamo...* Aeolian generations
are gone. Today I roamed on remote Filicudi:
painstaking drystone still terraces slopes they once farmed,
through crystalline blue sounds an occasional cock-crow;
in the high solitudes around Valdichiesa one man
buzzed shearing a track through a tangle of trees and weeds.

Road ends at a little shrine flaking pink and white,
and I sat there recalling how Sergio has told me
'Plenty from Filicudi have got rich out there.
They'll work eighteen hours, sleep on a sack of potatoes,
spend nothing in the shops. They just buy land.'
Sergio has sold his mini-market in Sydney

after thirty years, comes back to the islands
every April, staying through to October:
'I never see a winter's day.' Most never return.
I sat there thinking of things that are simple and sad,
beyond all to do with money. A path twisted on
to a whole collapsed village, foundered in vegetation.

Back down in the tiny port where I snacked by a palm tree
splayed like a mad windmill paralysed in mid-spasm,
forsaken homes are now the weekend bolt-holes
of well-heeled outsiders. In August they hold a Sea Festival:
where feluccas once rowed down swordfish, flower-decked vessels
laden with tourists process hearing songs of those scattered.

Dark matter astronomers term what is most of our cosmos,
unseen, known by its effects. Here on Lipari lights
still twinkle, each summer fisherman Franco can tout
for punters to boat round the islands, his friends rush from vineyards
to waiter in town, paint vacation-lets... Janet updates me:
'Oh, that place... Too much hassle. I sold it on.'

Broom in May

Again and again along switchback bends of coast road
I am hit with dizzying waves of the scent of broom
that draws me into itself, its great yellow blazons
on rock-face, sprawlings down drops to the sea,
it is like food, it assuages deep hunger. For what?

Creation puts forth its essence in scent and gold spillage,
and my mind climbs rungs to its attic lumber for apt
theologies, superstructures. None worth dusting-off:
they're at once excessive and insufficient.
The broom tells me nothing. Nothing I need not know.

The Donkeys of Alicudi

A corner of Earth forgotten at the moment
of Creation, left thus from the time of Chaos.

Having sailed overnight from Palermo,
its sumptuous coast of great villas and lemon groves,
Alexandre Dumas, drenching his trousers and shirt,
clambered ashore, for a couple of hours.
It is 1853; he can hardly believe what he sees:
In all the island there is neither a tree
nor scrap of vegetation to rest the eyes.
Only in cracks of the waste some stalks
of the heather which gave it its first name, Ericusa.
Yet on this chunk of lava in miserable huts
live 200 fishermen, trying to use the few patches
that have escaped the general destruction.

But where, Alexandre, are the donkeys?

Today there's a strip of concrete along from a jetty,
upon it a couple of cars. With nowhere to go,
there are no roads, and nowhere to build them:
at either end of a stony beach rock drops sheer into sea.
Lava-stone steps rear, houses perched off them.

When one lives in a certain world, in a certain manner,
there are lives, Dumas muses, *which are incomprehensible.*
What drew them to this spent volcano? Have they
just grown on it, like its heather?

These flat-roofed dwellings look solid enough,
are freshly whitened, have terraces tumbling flowers.
From one trots a child in a long pink dress
clutching a lemonade bottle: 'Ciao ciao!' she greets us.
She tells us a story about the Two Giants of Messina.
England she might find incomprehensible.

'But where,' you ask, 'are the donkeys?'

They are not working at present.
They work when a hydrofoil comes in, or a big ferry,
bringing what's needed. 'But look!'
you cry, and we scramble up over hummocks:
two of them, motionless in a tiny paddock,
accepting the shade of one tree.
They are like petrifactions, creatures fashioned from lava.
Their shoulders and backs are as high as my shoulders.
These are not donkeys for children's beach-rides,
nor meek like the ass that magnified Christ's humility
bearing him through the crowd to Jerusalem.
When not working they wait, on their long strong legs.
They have bred from each other for centuries.

'Don't go too close! One might kick you!'
But when I proffer my palm the nearer one swivels
its long and ponderous head, and sees there is nothing
for it to munch, and I see in its great soft eyes
resignation. It does not complain, or plead.

I have seen them standing patient down at the jetty,
as slap from our world a hydrofoil skims alongside,
to disgorge a few tourists, and crates, sacks, boxes.
When their backs are loaded, as they are twitched into motion
they unloose a long cacophonous braying
that resonates on and on as if powered by lungs of brass:
Oh yes oh yes oh we know we know what we are
what we're for oh yes as we have been for always
well why not, hurrumph.

This is not anguish, nor righteous indignation,
It is simple self-declaration. They plod-plod-plod
back up the steps, veering under their freight,
gentled along by occasional words from their owners.
Like them, knowing their place.

And now, as we wait by the ticket-office,
here they come, plodding down past us. Ten minutes before
our boat, an old woman hobbles along to unlock.
Behind the desk, her black eyes are ageless;
her fingers twinkle upon an electronic keypad.

United Italy

Traffic-lights, they say, in Milan give instructions,
in Rome they offer suggestions, in Naples they are
Christmas decorations. Here in the seven
Aeolian Islands there are no traffic-lights.

All flows, cutting corners, vrooming up alleys behind one,
passing wrong-side, threading strollers along the Corso
('closed' to vehicles at six; but where are the *carabinieri?*).
They are artists at last-second jinking to miss each other,

and you and me. Rosa lives in the narrowest *vicolo*
in town, her drying-rack leaves no way for the dinkiest
motorino; yet when she returns from work at the butcher's
(or sometimes the baker's, but now again at the butcher's)

the contraption's intact; and no one has stolen her knickers.
While up in Milan among gridlock and raging policemen
the *babygangster* swarm out of school to start mugging:
cellphones, designer clothes, keeping up with their peer-group.

Shirtless, pouring more wine (his children cavorting
outside where mountain shoulders the stars, and I wonder
how ever they get up for school), 'Never,' says Enzo,
'was Italy unified! 1861 was a Savoyard

putsch! Restore us our Bourbons!' (Northerners jested
that Sicily joining was less any unification
of Italy than the division of Africa.)
An ironist, Enzo may not mean his last sentence.

The Saint Protector

'That isn't *him*,' Janet nods towards him perched
over the harbour, 'They get shown doing something,
what they got sainted for, or how it was done to them,'
she pours more wine, 'Sebastian riddled with arrows,
or that female holding her eyes in a dish.
That's just some poser, I guess they found it some place
and designated it him.'
              Between the statue
(beyond it a hydrofoil furrowing white on blue water)
and our tables the strip of piazza is thronged,
'Ciao, Bartolo!' friend greets shoulder-clapping friend
as taxis and mopeds among them by miraculous
fractions evade collision.
              He has seen worse.
If he was ever him. Uncertain whether
his martyrdom was by flaying or beheading,
the tradition that he incurred it in Armenia
is a soufflé whisked up from nothing.
Outside the four apostles' lists he is
unknown to the New Testament, and as
the first syllable of the name means 'son of'
it is thought he may be the Nathanael
Jesus called, as 'an Israelite in whom
is no guile'.
        By the sixth century
St Gregory of Tours has a fancy yarn
about this son of Tolmai: *The pagans, seeing
people praying at his tomb, placed the body
in a lead sarcophagus and threw it in the sea;
but the waters carried it to an island called Lipari.
This was revealed to Christians so they could find it.*
It was a credulous time, and a sellers' market:
every place round the Mediterranean scrambling
for mummified remains of those who had died for Christ,
as Protectors, and advocates when Judgement sounded.
Other tales recount how his bones
were purchased from a vessel that called in,
or at an Eastern port.
            Be that as it may,
who better for an island people hauling

livelihood from the sea than one whose name
signifies 'son of he who moves the waters'?

Their devotion suffered setbacks.
Darae in Mesopotamia, and Phrygia,
staked their rival claims to the possession
of the sanctified Relics of Bartholomew;
and when in AD 729
~~Willibald (a brother to St Valpurga)~~
broke his journey back from pilgrimage
to the Holy Land to venerate them
he found the Protector groggy under the blows
of heavyweight nature: Monte Pilato in frenzied eruption
clobbering the island with pumice – and fled.
Then the Lombards filched the bones off to Campania.

Through all calamities the *liparoti* kept faith.
In 1544 they rang the alarm
from his bell-tower: *The Turks are at the Marina!*
Who sacked the town, and all they did not slaughter
were carried away into slavery.
The Spanish rebuilt (and round it, round their several
churches on what had once been the Greek acropolis
huge ramparts) the Cathedral of San Bartolomeo.
And every Good Friday, bearing regalia,
they process from it down and along the Corso.
I have stood watching from crowded pavement.

'The people here,' says Janet, 'are very superstitious,
they think if a cat breathes in your mouth you will die.'
As space clears before us: *'Juve! Juve!'*
all ages, in black-and-white waving chessboard flags:
Juventus are Champions! The infidel fans of Inter
are routed (till next time). This is the new religion,
cars circle honking.
                    Beneath him. Not his game.
Rather I see on the plinth a figure as of
a seasoned cricketer who, having taken knocks
from volcanic bodyline bowling, pirate raids,
seen off pitch invasions, stroked tourists to all
parts of the ground, tugs at his cap, and settles
to face the next ball, the next century.
                         'Ehi Bartolino!'
from the jetty where rope flies safe from boat to bollard.

Lava Flow

An incandescence
seared upon night
encrusted with stars.

Or, living and sinuous,
the gold-pithed tongue
of some ancient saurian
flickered forth
between summit and sea.

Of the greatest works
it has been said
you seem to overhear them:
the mighty transaction
of maker and matter
speaks to your inwardness.
Intimate as a star.

And this, if music
as Ezra Pound said is
pure form cut into time,
is Louis Armstrong's
trumpet in heaven.

What else should we do
as our boat bobs away
but, as happens, applaud? –
across our deck ripples
genteel handclapping.

But this is not art,
its performance not over.

Four months ago
the peak gouted ashes,
then the great landslide
beating up sea;
at the island's far side
it flung boats through houses,
a landfall of fishes.

And from the vent, magma:
when its tip touched blue water
steam shut off the sun.

They are back now
from evacuation,
the six hundred people
of Stromboli. Beneath
their *chiesa madre*
the piazza is empty,
tourists not coming.

Above, round the summit
buzzing all day,
a helicoper, waiting.

Conversation Piece

Before dawn I am woken by an immense ululation
of dogs, repeating an intricate litany
of yowls and responses, over the rooftops,
down alleys. What rough beast is slouching towards...?

I get up; and the sun also rises, to clarify fact:
my terrace tree is stripped of its thousands of apricots.
I shake rough boughs, not a fruit left to drop.
Thieves in the night, who must have brought sacks and a ladder.

The dogs would know nothing of this, they were just conversing.
My island friends lavish theories: that man last year...
Paola's mother has heard... Facts slither from grasp
like soap in the bath. More nutritious is conversation.

The Drift of Things

'Si è rotto,' shrugs Bartola, beaming,
the photocopier is broken; or it is the shower,

the phone, the computer, the car, the washing-machine,
last week two of Siremar's hydrofoils.

Trees along narrow pavements dangle
thorny clumps of foliage waist-low,

sashed swimsuited beauties posture on posters,
all raven-haired (I fancy *Miss Fascino*),

up for the title *Regina della Moda*
to be decided in August – last year.

Antonio, once the blond 'figlio d'oro',
is frazzled these days rushing from picking grapes

for his uncle to taking trippers out in his boat,
then late-night waitering at a *pizzeria*,

while ('HRH') Paola broods in the musical bar
('*Io cammino, a notte da solo,*

poi piango, poi rido'): how can she wangle a job
teaching Italian in those Scottish castles?

In Quattropani, centuries later,
they talk of their miracle, the Flying Madonna.

The phoenix could resurrect right under our noses,
or that *pasticciaccio*, that whole bloody mess in Iraq

take a turn from a spell transforming what gouts
from their oil-wells into tomato-sauce,

nothing would ruffle the drift of things in the Islands,
where volcanoes slumber or sputter, the sea winks back,

seagulls embroider cloudless blue
and breakfast coffee is always taken outdoors.

Manoeuvring below the pumice quarries
a truck churns up white dust-storm teeming with

the ghosts of half-naked children bearing their loads
down the blanched terrain, *'Gnuri, pi tri sordi.'*

Not long ago. And, 'Yes, the painting was taken
to the new building, but she flew back up

in the night, her footprint was found on the roof
of the Chiesa Vecchia. You see her there still.'

And tomorrow may come the technician, the plumber,
'Who knows?' – that we're-all-in-this-together smile.

Through surrounding darkness
I hear a chuckle of submarine gas-emissions.

Note: *'Gnuri, pi tri sordi'*, 'Signore, for three pennies'.

Freedoms

'Queen Victoria is dead,' Marisa informs me,
'your *regina madre*. I saw on our television.'
'Her name was Elizabeth.' 'No, that is your Queen.'
On Lipari, Victoria has just died.

Marisa's Canneto apartment has stereo equipment,
books, an exercise bike, an impeccable kitchen.
But she eats every evening, it is expected,
round at her parents'. If she does not, there are questions.
'My mother, in her time, until she was in her twenties
could not go out unchaperoned.'
Things change. But when Marisa worked in Messina
and might, on occasion, sip wine at the Bar Progressivo,
'People spread hurtful gossip back here round the island.'
Where Victoria's passing is belated.

Marisa has travelled: 'In England, to London and Cambridge.
To Paris. New York.' And the northern Italian cities.
'In those places I feel I have freedom.
I hate the Aeolians.' She means not her islands
('When I'm away I miss so much the light')
but, 'Everyone here knows everyone. Only, they don't.
I could sometimes napalm Canneto, leave just its buildings.'

Among which this morning up a stepped alley towards me
hobbled a crone in black with shopping; she turned
to unlock a blistering door, beyond her a gap
to seafront, bared flesh and parked cars.
She'll have done her bit. In her time. Had many children.

Nowadays even Italians who marry
neglect to have children. The birthrate has plummeted:
project from present statistics, and by the end
of this century they will be extinct,
bequeathing to our planet their wealth of great art.
'Have the third child!' the bishops are thundering;
but even a first, these days
so demanding and so expensive, cramps fulfilment.

'Oh, Marisa,' her mother can say, 'yes, she has a boyfriend,
a lawyer, no up in Milano, very respectable.'
Though scarcely a 'boy'. She likes, she tells me,
'to be a lot here on my own'.
Playing Jane Austen tapes to improve her English,
'And my painting.' She darts up the spiral of stairs,
brings down an armful. Some copies of modernist masters
and, in primitive style, white on bright blue,
seagulls exploding to freedom in every direction.

At Marina Corta

'... ma dimmi, perché assiso
quiritta se'? attendi tu iscorta,
o pur lo modo usato t' ha' ripriso?'

Dante, *Purgatorio 4*

A ruined gambler chancing one last throw
and landed here might count his lucky stars,
unpacking nightly over the island.

Reverberative hindsight. A snatch of song
lapping quiet as the water at its feet,
a spasm of remorse. Otherwise

along low harbour wall the figures postured
staring seaward or in towards the summit,
are mostly silent. One sits apart

cheek couched upon a palm; face-to-face
a couple rake the ash of their old quarrel;
others, exhausted, stretch out prone.

Lovelorn, she cherishes a mobile phone:
poor hurt bird, as if it might yet flutter
chirruping into new spring song.

And you, knees clasped, head down between them, turn
barely moving your face above the thighs:
'Climb it? A warm-up cripples me.'

Deliquescence of past negligences.
Within which how can we know what we wait for?
A new life. Taking pains.

Meeting Point

Like great stone quoits
lobbed onto this headland they
rest, weathered remnants
of a Bronze Age settlement.

A white sail in the cove,
the man on deck, cellphone
to ear, is talking
to Rome or Turin.

Could he, glancing up,
catch against sky that other
clutching spear or sling,
what meeting, beyond eyes?

Even in birth, sex, death
estranging etiquettes.
Need for small warmths, shared;
knowledge none last long.

Roast Lamb

'Pronta! Cheese!' Beside me on the top deck
she camera-clicks at the man on whom she was slabbering
sun-cream until, when we anchored and others went down
to the steps off the stern, he climbed the rail, postured,

then hippo-plummeted smashing the bay
half out of itself, and now he floats belly up
and limbs spread like a starfish in sea so clear
you follow the drop of cliff far underwater.

A whistle shrills recalling the swimmers,
and we are landed. I stroll from the little jetty
up to the church and piazza, around them a snaggle
of flat-roofed white dwellings, under the fuming summit.

Dusk congregates among bougainvillea, eating
swordfish I hear in that hybrid accent
I've come to recognise, 'Y'know what I mizz mose
back here in Stromboli? Izz the rose limb.'

'But surely,' the English couple he's talking to
at the next table demur, 'you have sheep in Italy?'
He swivels dark eyes at them: 'Yeah,
but nothing beats good old Aussie rose limb.'

He has prospered in Sydney, now returns as he pleases,
has bought his uncle's old house. The English
talk of prices, 'slow service', how 'In your pharmacies
they've not even heard of vegetarian toothpaste.'

And, 'The lizards, is their bite venomous?'
'A compatriot of yours' (deadpan) 'was chazed by one up a tree.
She was there for three days.' He offers them boat-trips,
vistas and grottoes. 'We'll see.' I doubt that they will.

Back on board I climb up onto the bow,
and after we've gazed up raptly at the explosions
of the volcano, when the engines start up
thrumming us through *la notte serena*

I talk with the girl from Palermo perched up beside me,
and her name is Serena, *la mia sirena siciliana*,
till a sprinkle of lights is Canneto, where she gets off,
and we round the long promontory to Lipari town.

In Via Garibaldi, wheeling her pram
is Alessandra from Ristorante da Bartolo
where last year, having walked over the heights
of Salina, I ate an enormous meal, and they wouldn't

take a *centissimo*, knowing it was my birthday.
Children still up are bouncing a ball, ice-creams
in their other hand, girls with bared midriffs stroll
under a moon hung low as the street-lights over the Corso.

'Sabenedica a Vossia, Don Bartolo!'
I hail the Captain in grovelling dialect.
He starts from his stool and doffs his *berretto*,
attempts a bow in response, but his girth prevents it.

He is dieting: 'Fruits! Salads!' the doctor orders,
which he eats, not instead of but in addition to
his chickens, pieces of fish, pastas, pastries, sauces.
Also he wants to improve his English:

he produces a sheet of paper on which is written
a phrase to attempt. He attempts it:
'The kikken is kikkin in the kikken...'
'No, not quite, Capitano. Try again.'

Within the shop Guy too waves a sheet of paper:
'Does one in English say "on the sea" or "by" it?'
In front of his counter a woman beams, sipping Coke.
'Olga asks I translate this advertisement

from her bastardised Russo-Italian, to put
on the Internet, to rent her apartment in Roma.
Which is rather, I think, her boyfriend's.' As well as her boyfriend
in Rome, she has one in Milazzo whom she makes take

her to Paris, much more expensive than Milazzo,
and a third, a bank clerk here. Who now rushes in:
'Coruzza mia!' 'Bastardo!' – she punches him out.
'Her apartment,' says Guy, 'she writes is by the sea,

yet in the mountains, and next to il Vaticano,
and all the other famous monuments.'
'Perhaps,' I suggest, 'you could say "*in* the sea".'
'Yes, and with Olga inside it!'

The Captain meanwhile has been working,
and getting it right at last he enunciates,
'The chicken is,' and adding a twist all his own,
'*cooking* in my kitchen! So, buona notte!'

I dodge the trees in the enclave before
my apartment, hear some fruit fall thwack! into grass.
'Roast lamb,' I murmur: these things
that I miss most when I am back in England.

Peccorini Mare

The smell of water drying on stones in sunlight,
a little quay, a few boats. Gazing from
the bar-restaurant terrace tucked beneath
greens and purples to the island's summit,

I've walked down hairpin bends straight into it:
that place, all my life along a turn
I didn't take or missed the sign for.
Throwing off enlarging rings

in my imagination. Or, on this
verdant dead volcano, is it merely
a refraction in my mind no years out there
can reach? No matter. Let it be.

Until my glass is empty, and I rise
and hoist my backpack. Start back up, in time.
Cric-cric-cric the cicadas are thrilling,
incessant and insistent, this last day of June.

2004

Still Life

Its juddering starts me awake, the whole apartment
and from my fridge a clattering of things in it,
a glass drops to smash on the kitchen floor
and by now I'm outside on my terrace…
A second tremor shakes the town under dawn sky.

And that is all. No buildings have fallen. This time.
By mid-morning the usual vendor is at
the far end of the Corso, up from Marina Lunga,
shouting his wares: 'Swordfish! Fresh swordfish!'
While in the Tourist Office Marisa is dealing

with Germans demanding, in their barking English,
'When will be your next earthquake? Will there be one
tomorrow? What time will it be at?'
She shrugs, she cannot tell them, watches them thinking
Ah, these Italians, so unreliable!

I take the hydrofoil, as it slows to Salina
I think of the many disasters come out of the blue:
the swagger of volcanoes and tidal waves, but also
the waves of human conquests. The caves where in vain
their women and children hid from slave-raiders.

Ciao ciao ciao today, as when pirates pulled in,
cry gulls, in greeting over the port.
Pink and white the Chiesa Madre faces
seaward, its hypertrophied dome
flanked by a bell-tower on each shoulder.

Along to the left is a slipway
upon which red and blue fishing boat hulls lie
tilted, aimed at where dawn sun lifts from water.
Still life I think, raising my camera.
Weathered through all seasons: *Hope at rest.*

A Leopardi of Lipari

'Your name, unless perhaps it is short for Gaetano,
is not Italian.'
    'I was named after my Uncle,
my famous Uncle.' He follows three customers
into his shop, to sell them cigarettes
or postcards, tissues, a comb, whatever they want,
returns to the doorway.
      'So how did it come about...'
'That he was named Guy? Before the First World War
my grandfather owned shops here in the Corso.
But seeking to make his fortune, he took the boat
to America, to Boston, Massachussetts.'
'Did he make his fortune?'
      'Oh yes, he prospered,
he and my grandmother, they owned shops in Boston.
But they couldn't stand the climate, after three years
they came back home, bringing with them my father
and my Uncle named Guy because he was born there.'
'What was he like, your namesake?'
      'He was a prodigy.
In Lipari then there was no electricity,
the schooling was basic, nothing to higher level.
By candlelight, in the cellar of our old house,
my Uncle taught himself literature, mathematics,
history and philosophy, the sciences,
and several modern languages including
Chinese and Russian.' More customers come in,
for Mars bars, film-rolls, cans of Red Bull beer,
an alarm-clock, one buys one of the huge posters
depicting sea gastropods.
    'And then?'
      'The Fascists
used Lipari as a prison island. Several
opponents of the regime were sent here, men
of culture, eminent socialists and artists,
and our *liparoti* were kind to them, having
no use for politics, which went on in Rome
remote as the wheeling of stars, and brought only afflictions,
they saw the poor exiles as fellow–victims of Fate.
But some of them chose to escape, they paid a fisherman

43

who took them off in his boat from the little beach
at Portinente. So then my Uncle,
the only intellectual on the island,
felt they had insulted the hospitality
of its people. He wrote a book about it.
It was not published.'
                              'And then?'
                                        'He emigrated.
Aged twenty he returned to the land of his birth.
But not to Boston, Massachussetts, but
California, where the climate is more like ours.'
'And did he prosper?'
                              'Yes, he was an inventor,
many creative things, and brilliant at business.
But among all this, he taught Russian, to the children
of Russian immigrants wishing their offspring to know
the mother-tongue, but unsure of its grammar.'
'So when you visited California...'
                                        'No,
I never met him. He went blind, and died young.
But a very old man, over eighty, possibly ninety,
when I was introduced to him, hugged me and cried
and kept shaking my hand, and wouldn't let go,
believing that I was Guy come back from the dead
after thirty years. I am perhaps something like him,
but lack his focus. I keep this shop open' –
it is 2 a.m., a girl, lustrous black hair
down to bare waist, enters, she wants a pen
that writes both black and red, for ticks and crosses,
she is a teacher, Guy shows her boxfuls,
also she buys a pack of Tarot cards
and a torch, and is gone, and he completes his sentence:
'... for social reasons.'
                              The Captain, who had dropped off
on his stool without dropping off, perks up, he tilts
grinning fatly: 'Or to make your fortune!'

Aeolian Sunset

In these latitudes, just left of the jut of crag
on this cliff edge, the blood-red disc drops fast upon sea,
you listen as if for a sizzle on touchdown,
and now it settles, half-sunk and all colour draining
from sky and water, the westerly islands are cindered,
and it is the merest sliver, then gone,
and within the engulfing darkness flare in my mind
the tatters of distant sunsets and figures of those
with me then, and also of those watched from this brink
by half-imaginable lives whose tomorrow
brought pumice raining down death from the volcano,
Saracen galleys to loot and enslave them, but mostly
just another day, behind a nail-plough,
cajoling mules up and down vertiginous track,
tossed in frail vessels spearing fish.
Still we, for whom tomorrow comes globalised
like acid-rain, on-screen the Twin Towers toppling
or Saddam's statue, the hosts of famine,
turn to it, the great orb that is our first parent,
and foster-parent to our sweetest illusions,
saying, *Let's watch the sunset.*

Summit Talk

'It is sunny today in Norwich, I have been playing
tennis, Christopher is basking in the garden.'
Sulphurous swirls from the Gran Cratere
catching my throat, 'They'll never believe that here,'

I gasp, 'they know in England it's always raining.'
I press *End call*, gaze out round a panorama
of the other islands, Sicily's north coast,
in mind's eye around the world.

Had the mobile phone existed in her time
Jane Austen's novels would not, all misunderstandings
pre-empted or sorted by page 30;
or a *hey-nonny* ring-tone in Juliet's placket,

'Romeo here...' – and, tragedy nutmegged, they
could have nagged each other for decades. Or in real life
Scott comes through: 'We're on our last legs,
but only a dozen miles from you at base-camp.'

Another waft: inward and down, the Inferno.
When the next jink of technology means we can talk
across time as well as space, it's you I'll call,
having the time of your life in the Afterlife,

hearing out those you respect, stashing Popes in a hole,
giving a kick in the chops to some wretch sunk in filth,
knowing sun and stars revolve round our 'threshing-floor',
and God has it all wrapped up:

Dante, your cosmology was moonshine;
history has binned your passionate hopes for it.
And your game is up, all your great show,
its pits and stenches, riven trunks, groans, monsters,

registering through your art as so
lived–through, seen and heard and terrifying,
is, after all, a bloody fairy-story...
In which, you knew, truth's 'hidden'; so disclosed.

The questions you raise trouble us still.
Today you'd hearken with much awe to Churchill
(plunged eternally in third-circle mire
for scoffing and boozing); be moved by

Marilyn Monroe (as once by flawed Francesca);
jabbering Hitler you'd pass with disdain.
But hell has burst from the confines you allowed it:
tell us in your indelible language

how we are in Iraq, the Sudan,
of our bankrolled tyrannies, gadgetries for killing
undreamt of in your Italy's squabbling fiefdoms;
as we strip Earth of its atmosphere...

I slither down sun-baked cinders to
the small port, an ice-cream. On their ledge of terrace
lemon trees teeter. *Don't jump...*
As if we'd talk ourselves back from the brink.

Gallimaufry

Nor is that all, round the bend into my garden I am downed:
science-fiction vegetation rears and claws me to the ground;

thorny fronds, entangling tendrils, when at last I struggle free,
minus shoes and glasses, hobble in and fumble with my key,

motionless as something shamming dead that gecko grappled high
underneath my terrace roof casts on me its evil eye.

'Paola came to my shop,' Guy told me, 'for cigarettes, dressed all in red
like the character in Perrault, a basket on her arm, she said,

"I'm away to the country to pick berries, see my grandmother."
That was seven days ago, I think the wolf has eaten her.'

Not that the Forest Guard will know, squandering round the harbour bars,
high above which glittering Orion hunts among the stars.

Moira, when you set the dial of your washing-machine to spin,
prancing from its niche door flapping frothily it gulps you in.

Rikkitina's trade is roaring, tables sprawl round her café,
amphorae from the Museum slop wine stomping there all day.

Propped on beach-towels staring up at screaming gulls' demented flocks,
helm-wheel whirling disconnected, helplessly we hit the rocks.

Once I had a secret love, the Captain beams as cracked and worn
Doris Day shrieks from his antique wind-up gramophone's huge horn.

Up at Lami buzzing flies enshroud the island's land-fill dump,
congregated scavengers for carrion grow sleek and plump.

Has a butterfly fluttered its wings in Timbuktu, the Philippines?
Google God and Mickey Mouse's websites clutter up our screens.

Cut to a cliff-top path, a fork, and choosing wrong again I miss
foothold as it narrows, steepens, plummeting into the abyss...

Waking from which, I get up, totter to my kitchen; through the wall
bursts the gecko, morphed into a dinosaur... Nor is that all.

Nocturne

Hands that trailed in peacock-blue water
over the stern of a boat, or held others' hands,

rest empty in sleep, in rooms spinning eastward
towards, but not yet, not yet, tomorrow.

The back-drag of dreams, great billowing
canopies painted with lost hopes, people.

And I am awake, staring into darkness
where silently vineyards and olive trees are fruiting,

at the harbour a hydrofoil chafes at its moorings.
The Dubliners sing in my ears:

But since it falls unto my lot, that I should rise, and you should not...
The wheels of the suitcase I trundle crunch over my heart.

The Captain's Swallow

Janet, she tells me, is painting swallows.
As I pocket my mobile Guy comes round from his counter:
'*L'artista americana*, so what of her mermaid,
her story she tells us for years that she works on?'
'I think it's not yet got its tail wet.'
                                    'But excuse me,'
il Capitano perks up on his stool, 'your word "swallow"?' –
he tilts his head, gulping ferociously. 'Yes, but also
the bird, *la rondine*.' Pino, who owns a volcano
in the south of the island, is watching us silently.
'Now in autumn,' says Guy, 'our swallows are all departed,
flown over Sicily to Africa, finding their way
right down to South Africa.'
                                    'But excuse me,'
eyes glinting, 'not all our *rondini* are departed.
One lives in my staircase.' He watches our faces,
white-haired Pino, who knows no English, stares mutely.
'It got lost and flew in. Would you like to see it?'

Guy is detained selling phone-cards as Pino and I
follow the Captain out, he unlocks his street-door.
Half-way up stone stairs on a thread of wire
on the wall, glossy black with a great forked tail...
'This *rondine*,' I declare, '*è morta*.'
'No no,' insists il Capitano, 'it sleeps.'
There isn't a flutter left in it. 'It's seen its last summer.'
Pino ducks his head to it, cocks an ear,
and pronounces: '*Respira*.'
He and the Captain nod to each other. 'Don't touch it!'
the Captain cries to me, 'you will frighten it!'
The pair shake hands. And I am no longer sure.
Here in the islands things are not what they seem;
except the volcanoes.

Two nights later the Captain again leads me up
his stairs, and points beaming: 'Look!' It is gone.
'It has flown off to join its friends in South Africa.'
He watches me cross the Corso, framed in his doorway,
burnished gold by stairlight...
                                    Along the coast

50

where cliff and sand are blanched from the pumice workings,
on the ramshackle jetty that staggers out into sea
under stars a mermaid sits combing her tresses.

Lewis Carroll in the Aeolian Islands

When I stepped off the hydrofoil
The Dodo pumped my hand:
'Here grapes grow huge as tennis-balls,
Our beaches are black sand,
In parts these seas are boiling hot.'
Why, this is Wonderland!

In shorts I wandered switchback tracks,
Cliffs, grottoes, heights, took stock
Of fumaroles wheezing among jags
Of red and ochre rock.
'Just the place,' I crowed, 'to hunt
The Snark or Jabberwock!'

The people go to bed at noon
Then stroll about all night,
Bump tumbling off their motorbikes,
And when the sun's so bright
None can be seen, shoot fireworks off.
'Their din's our chief delight!'

Vulcano's mud-pool's always thronged
Despite its frightful stink.
One woman thrust her bawling brat
Right under. With a wink,
'It benefits the health,' she said,
'He'll scrub back up to pink.'

There comes a rumble in the dark:
'The Red King snores!' they nod,
'We're all his dream, should he wake up...'
More buildings fall. Most odd.
Then all is clear: 'Cheer up!' I cry,
'It's just an Act of God!'

He moves here in mysterious ways,
　　Refreshing to report:
I saw a tidal-wave fling boats
　　To smash a little port,
And lava flows transform blue sea
　　To steam-cloud. Splendid sport!

One crater hurled out stuff that fell
　　Like hail, and lay feet thick,
'We call them breadcrust bombs,' declared
　　A motleyed lunatic,
'Take some home for your tea,' he urged.
　　They made me very sick.

Yet I'll no more of Oxford rains,
　　Dips in the freezing Isis;
Here I bask all day in heat
　　Ingesting water ices;
And, to occupy my brain
　　I turn to the World Crisis.

The War on Terror's on TV,
　　It's rather picturesque
(They censor out the flying limbs
　　As tasteless and grotesque).
I work the mathematics out,
　　Straw hat on, at my desk.

If ninety tanks with ninety guns
　　Shell two mosques for a year,
In logic... Yet invasion's sums
　　Won't come out right, appear
To multiply the terrorists.
　　The moral's very clear.

Being mad here keeps us sane.
　　I scale volcanic peaks,
Reach hand to bough for nectarines,
　　Fall in a trance for weeks.
The Cheshire Cat's grin comes and goes,
　　Knows all, but never speaks.

As I Walked Over

As I walked over the pass
between the twin peaks of Salina
the sun went out, the sky bruised across.

Sweetly at Leni the *campanile* chimed
the hour, four answering chinks
drifting faintly up from Rinella.

The downpour began.
Twenty hairpin bends and I reeled
into the little port,

the island purified to its primeval
self, rain lashing the shut *pizzeria*,
two cars like discarded trinkets.

'*No!*' croaked the crone in the ticket-office,
'*Tempo brutto! Mare forte!*
No hydrofoils will depart!'

I look back up: through infernal chiaroscuro
that shape detaching from
the vapours, wallowing down

as in clumsy flight, might be Dante's Geryon,
the scaly monster with clawed feet
and swingeing scorpion tail.

On a table a left-out glass of red wine
overbrims bleeding paler
and paler to the gutter.

As If There Were No Shadows

Merrily, suddenly merrily bells burst out ringing,
startling me to look up from my beer and along
over the throng, beyond San Bartolomeo
perched on his plinth, to the far end of the Marina:
the church cascading a tumult of melodies.

Easing limbs tired from so many switchback tracks
high in the island and never passing a soul,
I am slow to take in the drift, and to what
it gathers. But empty my glass, am drawn in.

By the ceramics shop stands a white vintage car
with two dark-suited attendants, red-carpeting runs
up the long stepped ascent to Chiesa San Giuseppe,
from the rails balloons ripple over the sea.
The pealing stops. Organ music. The service has started.

And people in shorts, in beachwear, are wandering in,
to stand at the back for a bit. As I do.
Now the priest is intoning, chill and crepuscular
as if from far intergalactic spaces.
Children beside me carry on eating ice-creams,
bounce balls, but out of respect refrain from their favourite game
of pushing each other about, or over.
At the front stand the couple, she is wearing a trailing white dress.
I go out, into sun so high there are no shadows.

At last all the casual wellwishers are ushered out,
and the congregation files forth, in their finery,
mingling among us, greeting relatives, friends.
And suddenly, there at the top, bride and groom.

She smiles and waves. There is an explosion
of shouts, released balloons, flowers thrown, confetti
flying like sea-spray, cameras clicking.
As they process down she swerves responding
to acclamations of 'Ahi, Bartola!'
The bell-tower bursts out in fresh rejoicing.
They walk straight past the white car
and ascend the humpy bridge that spans a slipway.

She makes a speech. More cheering. Dark-suited beside her
her husband shuffles, hangdog. They step down,
and turn among a bar-restaurant's tables.

Surely, after such ceremony, bells still pealing,
they're not just settling for a beer and sandwich?

'No no,' I'm told, 'her family own this café.'
Yes, tables are pulled together to one long table
heaped with food and wines; and how the families,
aunts, uncles, cousins, nephews, nieces, siblings,
some divorced, or barely standing each other,
and most having been unfaithful,
want all this for the pair on the threshold of adulthood
who've yet to meet most people it will bring them.
I think of the sadness of marriages.

She speaks again, thanks all, her black eyes flashing.
Now scissors flash, poor Bartolo's tie is cut off!
The white car sidles up. They both get in,
it glides eighty metres to the jetty,
a boat to the mainland, the airport, their honeymoon…

Hulked apart in the café, an old man,
swarthy, with silvered mane, a grandfather,
hunches into himself, contemplative,
like a chess grandmaster, or a gorilla.

While a tiny girl in a pink dress, clutching a yellow balloon,
twirls and twirls in purest happiness.

The light brilliant still. As if there were no shadows.

To the Observatory

The rail I lean on for the view back over
town and bay is so hot it would skin my palm,
and the road always rising, twists in it jinking from left
to right to left where I've come from, where I am heading.

Last night on the phone, 'Puoi sentire il mare?' I began,
waves lapping my shoes. Yes, you could hear it. We talked,
I imagined you moving. I like to watch you move.
Then suddenly I was foundering in your language:

Ti ubriachi I heard ('You make yourself drunk'),
which I wasn't. You said it again... Until, attuning
to my confusion, you found just enough English:
'I hug you.' 'Ah! – anch'io... Ti abbraccio!'

A final steep haul up, and the road ends beside
the Observatory tower. Groggy with sun,
boats tiny below me, and scarcely a stone's-throw across
the gulf the scaly rock-flanks of Vulcano,

what I see is the broad walk along the top
of those massive sea-fortifications in Sardinia
the week before we met last week in Taormina:
sweet shrilling overhead as I watched spellbound

sharp shadows flitting on the sunlit concrete
I walked upon, the thrilling interweave of it.
And some broke from the pattern, and skedaddled
up the fronts of buildings, vanishing at their rooflines.

Then I looked up, and never so many swallows,
unconstrained in their blue element
winging far out over sea, their lifts and glides
declaration that all's possible.

In the Picture

Familiar now to me as to generations
the high seaward jut of the Castello ramparts,
the drop from their cliff to the tall buildings
with narrow windows at this end of the Marina.

Today three boats, the spar for a look-out ahead
swung back from bluff prow over their hulls,
rest on the shingle, the one pulled highest empty
but for a slew of harpoons, the smallest half-hidden

by the third, in which two men in brimmed hats
are waist-deep behind the gunwale upon which stands
another, left hand on the mast (a leisurely stretch,
for neither is this a large vessel) for balance.

He is looking down at the man alongside
clad in the same hat and breeches, and two women
turned hands-on-hips to each other. Are they discussing
the price of swordfish? Is some intrigue going on?

In the foreground at the water's edge,
apart from it all but gazing at them intently,
stands a third woman also in a long dress,
her arms are cradling a baby.

What will happen next? Blows? Laughter? A kiss?
From such so near-at-hand our enlarging myths
are crafted, from brawls, births, jealousies, hagglings over
prices, should Homer or Aeschylus chance by.

While the boy, hands clasped behind back,
his back to them all, already booted and hatted,
who will never see us who are looking at him, stares
out into sea, into 1893.